"A racing car will tell
Unser things
that other
drivers can not
hear or
understand."

"interviews"

An Interview with
bobby unser

By John Gilbert
Photographs by Vernon J. Biever

CREATIVE EDUCATION/CHILDRENS PRESS

Published by Creative Educational Society, Inc., 123 South Broad Street,
Mankato, Minnesota 56001. Copyright © 1977 by Creative Educational
Society, Inc. International copyrights reserved in all countries. No part of this
book may be reproduced in any form without written permission from the
publisher. Printed in the United States.

Library of Congress Cataloging in Publication Data

Gilbert, John, 1942-
  Bobby Unser.

  SUMMARY: A brief biography of the race car driver who won the 1975
Indianapolis 500.
  1. Unser, Bobby—Juvenile literature. 2. Automobile racing drivers—United
States—Biography—Juvenile literature. [Unser, Bobby. 2. Automobile racing
drivers] I. Title.
GV1032.U57G54   796.7′2′0924 [B] [92]   76-42276
ISBN 0-87191-572-3

Bobby Unser has lived his life with the thunder of racing engines in his ears. He has lived with the feel of a straining racer ''talking'' to him through his fingertips as he guides it into a turn, death whispering to him just inches and a fraction of a second away.

His world is a racetrack. His goal is victory — being the first across the finish line. The rest of the world is a blur, whipping past on either side. He never sees it, never turns his head. The roar of crowds, even the 400,000 people who watch him at Indianapolis, and the screaming wind of his slipstream are deafening. He never hears them, never even notices them.

But Unser can hear the slightest change in pitch of a racer's engine. He can sense the slightest tremor, the first quivering indication of trouble.

He is like a machine himself, people who live in the world of auto racing say. A racing car will tell Unser things that other drivers cannot hear or understand.

His greatest pride is that he can get into any kind of a car on any track and drive it as fast as it can possibly go. And when they bury him, Unser knows what he'd like to have carved on his tombstone:

"That Bobby, he goes good wherever he races."

Unser's compulsion to win won't alone bring him a victory. Just driving fast and fearlessly won't do it either. "It takes pure concentration," Unser said.

"You've got to blank out everything else. Some people can do it; some can't.

"If I have a world war going on right next to me," Unser said, "I don't let myself notice it or think about it. Lordy no, I never take my mind off the race.

"Some drivers can't concentrate that well and they never make it."

Maybe Unser isn't the best racing driver in the world. There are so many different types of racing, so many different kinds of cars and tracks, and so many different rules that it would be impossible for any man to make such a claim. But Unser is one of the very best. No one who knows racing would argue with that.

In the fall of 1975 there was an attempt to settle that argument in a series called the International Race of Champions.

A group of identical cars, engineered and built to exactly the same specifications, was provided. Then top drivers from all over the world — from Indianapolis, the stock car circuit, the European road racing circuit — came together.

The drivers drew lots for cars and then raced in identical cars, under identical conditions, on the same track, with the same pit crews. The only difference was in the driving. There were a series of preliminary races. The top point-getters then were matched in a championship race.

Unser won that race.

"It was one of the pinnacles of my career, no doubt," he said. "But I'm not saying it necessarily means I'm the best driver. It does probably make a lot of people look at me and say, 'That Bobby, he goes good wherever he races.' "

"I never set
goals for
myself...

If I had,
maybe I
wouldn't
have set
them **high**
enough..."

If an artist were told to draw a picture of a typical cowboy — what most Americans think a cowboy should look like — he'd probably come up with something like Unser.

Bobby is tall, about 6-feet, 1-inch, and lean. His eyes are blue and his features are angular, even hawklike. His blond hair would be curly if he let it grow, but he keeps it cut short. He talks the way he drives — fast, but in the flat twang of the western plains where he was born and still lives.

A century ago Unser would have been a cowboy. His instincts would have driven him toward the challenges of frontier life. But the world of racing was being opened up when he was born. His father, Jerry, and two uncles were pioneer racers. Bobby's three brothers, Jerry Jr. and Louie, who were older, and Al, five years younger than Bobby, were all drawn into racing at an early age.

"I was born in Colorado but we moved to New Mexico when I was too young to remember," Unser said. "I drove my first car when I was 10.

"Not on the roads of course. But we lived where we've got hundreds and hundreds of miles of who-knows-what, just flat land on all sides of our house. We learned to drive on that land.

"Al and I still own land and have houses there, one on each side of the road. It's still pretty wild country. As kids, we used to catch wild horses in that country.

"All four of us boys wanted to race. I don't know exactly how the idea got started, but probably because my dad and uncles were racing sprint cars and modifieds."

Sprint cars are older cars like those that raced at Indianapolis years ago. They're still popular on dirt tracks all over the country. A modified racer is one you build by taking an automobile body and dismantling it. You rebuild it to be lightweight and use a big powerful motor.

"When I was 15, I had my first race. It was in a super-modified at Cormit Speedway in Albuquerque. My father wasn't racing then, but he owned five race cars and one day one of the drivers didn't show up. He let me drive it and it turned out to be the fastest one of the five.

"The car was a 1931 pickup truck cab with a LaSalle engine. I don't remember how I did in that first race, I think fourth or sixth. But Daddy let me keep driving it and the next year I won the Southwestern Championship. Got a trophy to prove it.''

At 16 Bobby became a hero of sorts in his high school. He didn't enjoy it.

''The English teacher used to tease me in school the day after I'd win a race. She used to make me stand up because my picture had been in the paper and all the kids would clap. I thought that was pretty stupid.

''I completed my sophomore year in high school and then I quit. I thought it was a big joke. But I don't believe that way now. I'll tell you one thing, school was a lot easier than doing what I tried to do.

''I raced on what they called the outlaw circuit. It was unorganized and the rules on what you could do to the engines weren't real strict.''

What Unser meant was that there weren't any rules except those that promoters made up. They would set up races to attract large crowds, which meant the more thrills the better. If a promoter happened

to own a car himself or had a deal going with an owner, he would fix the rules to favor his car or his friend's.

It was a hard and dangerous life for a teenager like Unser. He'd make his way around the country any way he could. When he got to a track, he'd look for an owner who hadn't signed up a driver and make the best deal he could. Usually it was for a share of the winnings, if any. Sometimes a beginning driver had to pay an owner to drive in an outlaw race and hope he would win enough to get his money back or maybe a little more.

Unser didn't get the best cars in those years. He got whatever was left over. He lived on hamburgers and chili and slept wherever he could, sometimes in a room with six or eight other drivers and mechanics. They would sleep "cowboy style — with backbones for mattresses and their bellies for blankets."

But Unser learned his business. He took risks that would knot a man's guts and turn his own hair white if he thought about them now. He got the reputation of being able to get the best out of any car under any conditions — and maybe just a little bit more.

"That Bobby, he goes good wherever he races."

Owners of the top cars began signing him to drive. "I was winning and having a good time," Bobby said, "and I had become desirable for promoters, so they paid me 'deal money' under the table to show up at their tracks." Unser started driving in bigger, more important races.

"I never set goals for myself," he said. "If I had, maybe I wouldn't have set them high enough and maybe I would never have done what I've done. But when I was growing up, my greatest desire was to win the Pike's Peak Hill Climb.

"The road up to Pike's Peak (near Colorado Springs, Colorado) is beautiful — all ground-up granite rock. It crosses valleys and canyons and winds for 12½ miles before you get to the top. My dad and his brothers raced at Pike's Peak. They put the first motorcycle and side car in history on the top of Pike's Peak before there was a road.

"So Pike's Peak meant a lot to our whole family and I wanted to be king of the mountain. It was almost an obsession from boyhood."

In 1955, when he was 21, Unser made his first run at the mountain. He finished fifth, but the next year he won the race. Eventually he was to win it 12 times. He was "King of the Hill."

When Bobby wasn't winning that mountain race, it seemed that another member of the family was. His uncle Louie won it nine times, and his brothers Al, Louie, and Jerry each won it twice.

Unser is especially proud of his brother Louie, who suffers from a disease that attacks the nerves and affects coordination.

"Louie came down with multiple sclerosis," Unser said. "We noticed it when he was racing. He started to lose his balance. He wrecked a car at Pike's Peak one time and we knew he shouldn't have wrecked the way he did. In checking back, they discovered he had multiple sclerosis.

"But Louie just went on with life. He became one of the biggest morale boosters for other people who have the disease. He doesn't let it bother him and he gets along just super. When he couldn't race anymore, he became one of the leading engine-building mechanics around.''

When he was 21, Bobby took over his father's business, an auto repair garage. He kept racing for fun and a few years later realized that it could be a profitable career.

"In 1959 I bought my own race car with money I had made from racing, and won with it. I realized racing paid a little if you won, so I bought myself an airplane. Then I was able to get around to races in California and other places. The airplane supported racing, because I could get to a lot of them, and I'd win enough to support the plane. I broke just about even, but every year Pike's Peak would come around and I'd make myself a little profit that would hold me over till next year.''

People kept urging Bobby to enter the Indianapolis 500 race, but he wasn't interested. It had tragic memories for him.

"My brother Jerry (Louie's twin) was the national stock car champion in 1957, but he died in 1959 in an accident at Indianapolis . . . he died, but he also was a champion before his crash so he accomplished something few people do.

"Still, Indy didn't seem like my bag," Bobby said, "not with those memories of Jerry."

Then Parnelli Jones, a famed racing driver, persuaded Bobby to drive at Indianapolis. It is, Jones pointed out, the most famous race in the world. The winner can earn more than $100,000 in prize money and make much more from endorsements and for personal appearances. A driver as good as Unser owed it to himself and to the sport to enter, Jones said.

"Parnelli found a car for me to take my rookie test in," Unser said, "but I couldn't make it go fast enough and I think I wrecked it once anyway."

Unser isn't kidding when he says he "thinks" he wrecked that car. He has driven so many races, so many cars, so many tracks that they all seem to blur together. He finds it hard to remember one wreck from another, one car or one track from the other. Other drivers tease him about it.

"The worst I ever got hurt," Bobby said, chuckling, "was from playing around, not on a race course.

"A race car driver
doesn't have a coach...
He's his own best asset
or his own worst enemy."

"A friend had a go-kart with two engines . . . We were on a big factory parking lot and I was going around in circles. The little thing had a lot of power. But all of a sudden, one engine stalled and then the other. The thing swerved and was out of control at high speed.

"I could see I was heading for a car and would have gone right under it. That would have cut me in two, so I turned and hit a cement block building head-on.

"That was the last thing I remembered for a long time. They tell me the go-kart was wrecked so bad they just picked it up and dropped it into a trash can."

They almost did the same thing with Unser. It took him a year to recover fully.

"I had a lot more bad years than good years," Bobby recalls, "but when you look back, you don't remember the hurts. I was in the 'crash house' quite a few times and I've got a lot of scars. I probably spent a total of two years in hospitals if you add it all up . . . but even the bad times seem like good times now."

It is difficult to compare racing drivers with other

athletes, Unser said. The physical strain of driving is terrific, but it is as much mental as it is physical.

"In football or baseball or other sports," he said, "you've got somebody to tell you when to eat, sleep, do push-ups, throw the ball — everything. A race driver doesn't have a coach like that. He's his own best asset or his own worst enemy.

"I stay in good enough shape to get the job done. Some drivers train harder than others. I used to horse around lifting weights a little. I ride motorcycles off-road and dune buggies, and I hunt and do some things like that. Also, I ride snowmobiles a lot.

"Some football players train hard but can't make it through the whole game. But look at somebody like Mario Andretti. He weighs only about 135, but I've never seen him fall out of the seat of a race car yet. Now, A. J. Foyt is built like an oversized fireplug. He would have made a heck of a football player because he's solid muscle. But I've never seen Foyt wear down Mario in a race.

Unser doesn't wear down either, but his other strengths as a racer can sometimes turn on him. Unser thought of the 1975 Indy 500, which he won.

"Bobby Unser
doesn't
care how far
ahead
he is,

just so he
crosses
the
finish line
first."

He was speeding down the back straightaway on the 175th lap, his concentration only on driving, when the radio receiver in his helmet crackled with a message from his pit crew.

"Dan Gurney came on the radio and said it was raining. I didn't understand because I was heading into the third turn and there was no rain where we were. But by the time I came into the fourth turn to come onto the main straightaway, I could see that it wasn't raining, it was POURING!"

Racing cars have fat, slick tires. They are designed for maximum traction on a smooth track. The slightest bit of moisture is dangerous. The tires lose their grip. And that cloudburst was turning the Indy track into something like a river.

"We all slowed down," said Unser, "probably to about 70 or 80. Even at that speed, I couldn't see anything. My helmet visor was covered with water so I flipped it up, but the raindrops burned my eyes and that was worse."

When they hit the water, the cars began to spin and crash and crunch into each other. It was like a dodge-em track at an amusement park. Fortunately, they had all slowed sufficiently to prevent any fatal accidents.

Officials stopped the race and declared Unser the winner.

"I was glad they stopped the race when they did," he said, ". . . but we would have won it regardless because we were far enough ahead. It would have been a close finish maybe, but the race I won at Indy in 1968 was closer.

"A lot of people say that 1968 race was the best one they've ever seen at Indianapolis. There were no restrictions like the fuel limitations in later years, so we just raced all day, as fast as we could go — flat out."

That race went the full 200 laps and Unser led 117 of them. But his big opposition came from three turbine-powered racers entered by Andy Granatelli. Racing people called those whirring engines the "silent screamers." Unser drove a piston-engine car.

"But a little pin vibrated out of position on my gearshift lever," Unser said, "and it left me with only fourth gear (the highest) in my car. That was fine on the straightaways, but it meant that I had to creep out of the pits very slowly when I stopped.

"Once I got on the track and up to speed, I could blow the turbine off like it was parked. I was running laps 1½ seconds faster than the turbine all day."

Still, because of Unser's gearshift problem, a turbine racer had the lead with 10 laps to go. Then the turbine broke down and Unser roared to victory.

Either way, Unser said, he would have won that race. "Once I hit the turbine's slipstream, it would take me only one straightaway to get past him. At the rate we were both going, I would have caught up to him on the white flag lap."

The white flag is waved to indicate that one lap remains. If Unser's calculations were correct, that would have been the closest race in Indy history.

And that would have been all right with Bobby Unser. He doesn't care how far ahead he is, just so he crosses the finish line first.

creative education

"interviews"